Kwanzaa

ABDO
Publishing Company

A Buddy Book

Published by Buddy Books, an imprint of ABDO Publishing Company, 4940 Viking Drive, Suite 622, Edina, Minnesota 55435. Copyright © 2003 by Abdo Consulting Group, Inc. International copyrights reserved in all countries. No part of this book may be reproduced in any form without written permission from the publisher.

Printed in the United States.

Edited by: Christy DeVillier
Contributing Editors: Matt Ray, Michael P. Goecke
Graphic Design: Denise Esner
Image Research: Deborah Coldiron
Cover Photograph: Picturequest
Interior Photographs: Comstock, Corbis, Photodisc, Picturequest

Library of Congress Cataloging-in-Publication Data
Murray, Julie, 1969-
  Kwanzaa/Julie Murray.
    p. cm. — (Holidays. Set 1)
  Summary: An introduction to the history, purpose, and observance of Kwanzaa.
  Includes bibliographical references and index.
  ISBN 1-57765-955-4
    1. Kwanzaa—Juvenile literature. [1. Kwanzaa. 2. Holidays.] I. Title.

GT4403 .M87 2003
394.261—dc21

                                    2002027751

Table of Contents

What Is Kwanzaa?

At one time, the word **holiday** meant "holy day." Many holidays are tied to religion. A few religious holidays are Christmas, Hanukkah, and Diwali.

Some holidays are not tied to religion. One of these is Kwanzaa.

Kwanzaa celebrates family, community, and culture.

During Kwanzaa, African-Americans celebrate their **culture**. They honor the history and **customs** of their **ancestors**. African foods, stories, and gifts are all part of Kwanzaa. People in Europe, South America, and the Caribbean celebrate Kwanzaa, too.

Kwanzaa lasts for seven days. It begins on December 26th and ends on January 1st.

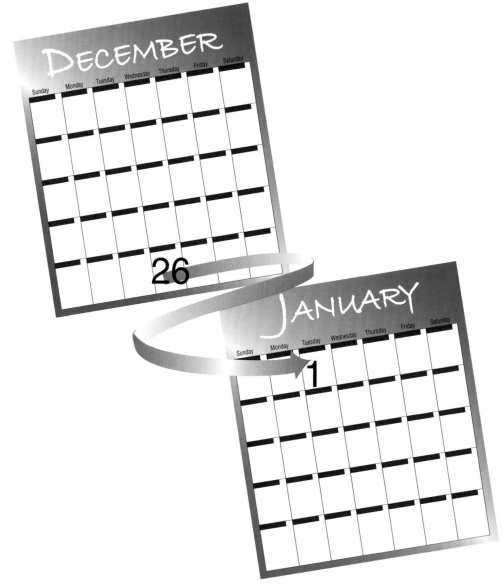

How Kwanzaa Began

Dr. Maulana Karenga started Kwanzaa in 1966. He wanted African-Americans to be in touch with their

history. He believed Kwanzaa would build strong African-American **communities**.

Dr. Maulana Karenga is a teacher at California State University, Long Beach.

A postage stamp honoring Kwanzaa.

Dr. Karenga had studied African **harvest** festivals. Celebrating family and **community** was an important part of these festivals. Dr. Karenga built Kwanzaa upon these African **customs**. Kwanzaa is full of African beliefs and values.

Swahili is an African language. Speaking some Swahili words is part of Kwanzaa. The word *kwanzaa* is Swahili, too. It comes from *matunda ya kwanza*. This means first fruits of a **harvest**.

Setting out fruits and vegetables is a Kwanzaa custom.

Seven Principles Of Kwanzaa

Principles are rules to live by. Every day of Kwanzaa celebrates a principle, or value. Kwanzaa's Seven Principles are called *Nguzo Saba* in Swahili. The Seven Principles are:

 *Umoja,* or Unity

Unity is a feeling of togetherness. *Umoja* is about keeping unity in families and **communities**.

Kujichagulia, or Self-determination

Self-determination is about making choices for yourself. *Kujichagulia* is about choosing whom you want to be. It is about choosing your future.

Ujima, or Collective work and responsibility

This principle is about working together as a group. *Ujima* means helping others in your **community**.

Ujamaa, or Cooperative economics

Ujamaa means sharing with others. It is also about helping community businesses.

 *Nia,* or Purpose

Having a purpose is like having a goal in life. *Nia* is about the goal of building a stronger **community**.

Kuumba, or Creativity

It takes creativity to think of new ideas. *Kuumba* is about finding new ways to improve your community.

Imani, or Faith

Faith is belief and trust. *Imani* is about believing in yourself and in others.

Kwanzaa Colors

Black, red, and green are important colors for Kwanzaa. Black stands for African-Americans and all people of Africa. Red stands for their struggles. Green stands for hope and the future.

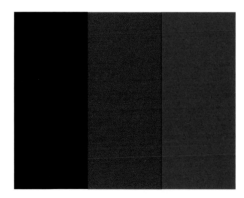

The colors of Kwanzaa are black, red, and green.

Kwanzaa Customs

Setting special items on a table is one Kwanzaa **custom**. Each item has a special meaning.

The *mkeka* is a straw mat. It stands for history and tradition. On the mat are fruits or vegetables. They are called *mazao*. The *mazao* stand for hard work and the **harvest**. *Muhindi* are ears of corn. *Muhindi* stand for children. There is one ear of corn for each child in the family.

A Kwanzaa unity cup

The table for Kwanzaa holds a wooden cup, too. This is the *kikombe cha umoja,* or unity cup. Everyone drinks from the unity cup. They say *"Harambee."* This means, "Let's all pull together."

Giving small gifts is another part of Kwanzaa. These gifts are called *zawadi*. Homemade Kwanzaa gifts are common. They are meant to teach about African **culture**.

Children may receive special gifts during Kwanzaa.

The Kinara

The special candleholder for Kwanzaa is called a *kinara*. It stands for a family's **ancestors**.

A *kinara* holds seven candles. Each candle stands for one of the Seven Principles. Someone lights a candle each day of Kwanzaa. Then, everyone discusses the principle for that day.

A *kinara*

Swahili Word Guide

Use this guide to help you read and say Swahili words.

a = the **ah** sound in "father"

e = the **ay** sound in "play"

i = the **ee** sound in "tree"

o = the **o** sound in "no"

u = the **oo** sound in "zoo"

harambee....hah-RAHM-bay

imani ....ee-MAH-nee

karamu ....kah-RAH-moo

kikombe cha umoja
..................kee-KOM-bay chah oo-MO-jah

kinara ....kee-NAH-rah

kujichagulia....koo-gee-chah-goo-LEE-ah

kuumba ....koo-OOM-bah

matunda ya kwanza

 ....mah-TOON-dah yah KWAHN-zah

mazao ....mah-ZAH-o

mkeka ....mm-KAY-kah

muhindi ....moo-HEEN-dee

nguzo saba ....nn-GOO-zo sah-BAH

nia ....nee-AH

ujamaa............oo-jah-MAH-ah

ujima ....oo-JEE-mah

umoja..............oo-MO-jah

zawadi ....za-WAH-dee

Kwanzaa Today

A big meal, or *karamu*, happens on December 31st, or the sixth day of Kwanzaa. People often bring African foods to share. Some favorites are black-eyed peas, okra salad, sweet potato pie, and benne cakes. Benne cakes are sweets with sesame seeds. They stand for good luck.

Sweet potato pie may be one of many foods at a Kwanzaa karamu.

This family has set up a special table for Kwanzaa.

Family and friends gather together for the *karamu*. They celebrate with music, dancing, gifts, and stories. Telling stories about **ancestors** is common. Children also learn about great African-American leaders.

Millions of people celebrate Kwanzaa each year.

During Kwanzaa, people look back on their lives. They remember their achievements. They also think about what to do for the future. Celebrating Kwanzaa helps people prepare for the new year.

Important Words

ancestor family members who lived long ago.

community a group of people who have something in common. People of a community commonly live near each other.

culture the arts, beliefs, and way of life of a group of people.

custom a practice that has been around a long time. Eating benne cakes is a custom of Kwanzaa.

harvest what is gathered from ripe crops. A harvest may be vegetables, fruits, or grains.

holiday a special time for celebration.

Web Sites

To learn more about Kwanzaa,

visit ABDO Publishing Company on the World Wide Web. Web site links about Kwanzaa are featured on our Book Links page. These links are routinely monitored and updated to provide the most current information available.

www.abdopub.com

Index

6/05　2　1/05

12/14　⑧　7/15